Spilling the Beans on...

Charles Darwin

and a selection of others (naturally)

First published in 2000 by Miles Kelly Publishing,
Bardfield Centre, Great Bardfield, Essex CM7 4SL

Reprinted 2001

Printed in Italy

British Library Cataloguing-in-Publication Data
A catalogue record for this book is available from the
British library.

ISBN 1-902947-64-9

2468109753

Cover design and illustration: Inc
Layout design: GardnerQuainton

Spilling the Beans on...

Charles Darwin

and a selection of others (naturally)

by Dennis Hamley

Illustrations   Mike Mosedale

ABOUT THE AUTHOR

Dennis Hamley lives in Hertford with his wife and their two cats. He has a son who is a scientist, a daughter in publishing and a grandson.

He has written many children's books. *The War and Freddy* was shortlisted for the Smarties Prize. He writes mysteries for a children's crime series, including *Death Penalty* and *Deadly Music*, and is now writing six mysteries set in the Middle Ages. He also writes football, ghost, animal and railway stories.

He often visits schools for talks and he also runs creative writing courses.

CONTENTS

CONTENTS

CHAPTER ONE

What did people think before Darwin?

Darwin? Who's Darwin?

It's a long story. First of all, here's a simple question. Where do you come from?

No, I don't mean, "I come from Ashton-under-Lyne," or even Stow-on-the-Wold. I mean – where do you as a human being come from?

No, I don't mean, "I was found under a gooseberry bush," or "the stork brought me," or even how it really happens (though we won't go into that now).

I mean, where do you as a *human being* come from, as opposed to where do you as a three-toed sloth come from, or where do you as a duck-billed platypus come from?

Well, I come from apes, don't I? They're the nearest to human beings. Some learned to stand up straight, use their hands, make tools, speak, put clothes on, and there you go – US. Not bad. BUT – if I'd asked you that question at any time before 1859, what would you have said?

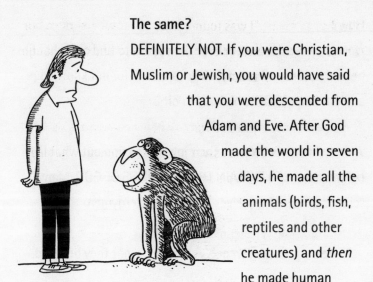

The same?

DEFINITELY NOT. If you were Christian, Muslim or Jewish, you would have said that you were descended from Adam and Eve. After God made the world in seven days, he made all the animals (birds, fish, reptiles and other creatures) and *then* he made human beings to be their masters. But Adam and Eve messed up in the garden of Eden, and we've regretted it ever since.

There's no time now to go into what you would believe if you weren't Christian, Muslim or Jewish.

Just a minute. Why did you say 1859?

Because that's when Charles Darwin published his great book, *The Origin of Species.*

Yes, but what about scientists before 1859? They didn't believe that, did they?

Yes. They saw things differently then.

How?

Nowadays – scientists believe their job is to find out what lies behind nature and use it if they can, both for our knowledge and our benefit. Or to blow us to bits.

Then – scientists believed their job was to find out what lay behind nature TO EXPLAIN THE WORKINGS OF GOD. Many scientists were themselves priests and clergymen.

There's a great difference. And here's what they believed.

a) The Earth, according to the Bible, was about 6,000 years old.

b) It had been made the way God designed it and had not changed. Nor would it.

c) All species were fixed. So three-toed sloths came into the world as three-toed sloths and three-toed sloths they would remain. The same applied to duck-billed platypuses. They had been like that for all time and that's how they would stay. This rule was so important that it was given a name –

THE IMMUTABILITY OF SPECIES.

Immutability?

Yes. Incapable of change. And why couldn't they change?

BECAUSE GOD CREATED THEM.

So there they were, all those prosperous people in the
19th century. They believed that nothing would ever change.
They believed that they as human beings were special. God
had created them separately from all other living beings. The
world was like a great league table.

1. God.
2. Angels.
3. Mammals (including human beings).
4.
5. } *Absolutely everything else in the world*
6. } *to infinity.*
7.

I reckon that if you could be sure of that, then you'd feel pretty good.

I suppose so. Did they?

Oh yes. As the 19th century got started, people really felt confident. Why, they knew nearly everything there was to be known. They'd explored most of the world. They'd found animal and bird species thay had never heard of and were on the look-out for more.

They'd found savage tribes which needed civilizing. Who better to do it than your English 19th-century gentleman? After all, who was more civilized than him? A good reason to conquer half the world and call it your empire.

Besides, they had steam engines and great factories full of machinery. They could do pretty well anything they wanted to – so they thought. Why, one day they might even learn how to fly.

Oh, yes, they felt GREAT!

THEN ALONG COMES DARWIN AND SAYS, "IT'S NOT LIKE THAT AT ALL".

Well, what would you feel?

Gutted?
Probably. But would you believe it?

I wouldn't want to.
No, you wouldn't. Especially as it seemed to deny that God existed.

Well, doesn't it?
What do you think? It all depends on how you read the Book of Genesis about how the world was made. The Bible and Darwin can't *both* be right.

Or can they?

You tell me.
Later, later. Meanwhile, this is the battleground. Is it CREATION? Or is it EVOLUTION?

Evolution? What's that?

When things change and develop over a very, very long time.

So what's creation?

When things come into being separately, caused by a maker.

Evolution must mean that all life started from the same source – probably a tiny microbe in the mud when the Earth first began.

Creation certainly means that each being was made separately, with a purpose and as part of a great design.

EVOLUTION versus CREATION. Which was it to be?

CHAPTER TWO

*   *   *   *

Who made Charles Darwin?

His mum and dad, of course.
I know. But here's the first hint of what evolution may be.

Meet: On his father's side – ERASMUS DARWIN.

A very fat man. And brilliant as well. He was into everything: fascinated by the new canals, the first steam engines. He even wondered if all he'd been told about how God made the world and all the animals was really true. In 1796, 15 years before

Charles was born, he wrote a book – *Zoonomia*. In it, he worked out his ideas. Some people thought these ideas were mad, others that they were bad. Just a few thought they were wonderful.

But the time for these ideas had not yet come. Besides, they were only ideas. He had no proof and didn't know where to get it from.

Meet: On his mother's side – JOSIAH WEDGWOOD.

Ever heard of Wedgwood Pottery? Have you been to Stoke-on-Trent? Not just the home of Sir Stanley Matthews, the famous footballer, but of china cups, saucers and dinner plates as well.

Josiah started it. In his Etruria Works he organized almost the first factory run on modern lines. Soon the 19th century would be full of industrialists like him. And the 20th, and the 21st – maybe.

So there we are. Two men years before their time, not afraid to change things and think for themselves.

Two generations later, Charles combined the qualities of both. That, very shortly, is what evolution is. Erasmus's son, Robert, married Josiah's daughter, Susannah.

Robert was a doctor and they settled in Shrewsbury. Robert was also a financial whizz-kid. Nowadays, he'd have gone to the City and made millions. Instead he stayed at home doctoring, investing his money and helping people into business. That was the time to do it. The Industrial Revolution was definitely on and there were fortunes to be made.

No wonder he had lots of patients. They might not get better but they could get rich. And Robert did too. Lucky for Charles.

Robert and Susannah had three daughters, Marianne, Caroline and Susan. Then came a son, Erasmus, named after his grandad. At last, in 1809, when Susannah was 44, Charles was born.

Forty-four? That's old, isn't it?

She had another baby, Catherine, 15 months later. You wait till you see how old Charles's wife was when she had their last baby. It wasn't much fun being a married woman in the 19th century. It wasn't a load of laughs being single either. In fact, it was best to avoid being a woman at all.

Now I come to think of it, Charles Darwin changed all that, too, though he didn't mean to.

★   ★   ★   ★

CHAPTER THREE

A lab in the shed

Was Charles a clever child?

Far from it. More of a pain in the neck. He was an attention

seeker. He broke things. He was jealous of little Catherine. Once he got on everyone's nerves so much that they locked him in a room as a punishment. But he tried to smash the windows. Caroline, his big sister, was supposed to look after him, but he was a real handful.

Why Caroline?

Susannah was ill. When Charles was only eight, she died. In those days, children weren't supposed to show grief. He bottled it all up. It changed him.

How?

He started collecting things. Anything – stones, shells, you name it.

He wanted praise, especially from his father. He never got it, so he just collected more things. The family had a greenhouse. Charles spent hours among the plants. They kept pigeons and he spent hours with them as well. Nobody guessed this was how he would spend most of his later life. His father decided he needed company his own age. It was time for him to go away to boarding school.

To Eton or Harrow or somewhere a long way off, I suppose.
No. Shrewsbury.

But he lived there already.

Even so, they sent him off to board there with his elder brother Erasmus. His father seemed to think this was a good idea. Charles definitely did not.

Shrewbury school was then a very small, very old place. It had a fierce headmaster, Dr Butler. There was no English taught (why should it be – everybody spoke English!); no science; a little maths. Most of the time was spent learning Latin and Greek.

Why?

Because that, Dr Butler believed, was how you became a cultured gentleman able to rule the country and also the world.

Sounds weird.

Maybe it does, but that's what public schools believed for the next century-and-a-half. People thought Dr Butler was a really way-out teacher of the future.

What was Charles like at Greek and Latin?

He *HATED* them. He longed to be back home. His brother Erasmus had fitted up an old garden shed as a lab. Here, in the holidays, they did experiments together and went on long expeditions looking for strange plants and weird insects. Then they learnt what they were and how to name them.

Yes, this was where he got his education, not school.

Why, what did finding out insects' names teach him?

It taught him habits of care and precision. The more he found, the more he wanted to know.

He sounds like a bit of an anorak. He'll be collecting Eddie Stobart lorries next.

Even if lorries had been invented, I doubt that. He was learning to be a 19th-century scientist. Collecting, naming, finding out. That's what science was then. There were so many new species to find, to identify. It's just as well they did. Half of them have since disappeared.

So he was going to be a scientist, was he?

Not yet. Charles was a great disappointment to his father.

Dr Darwin thought his second son was a bit thick. Still, there
was one thing he could probably do.

BE A DOCTOR!

Erasmus was already at Edinburgh University training to be
one. If Charles went up to join him, Erasmus would keep him
out of trouble and help him with his studies.

So Charles went to Edinburgh.

CHAPTER FOUR

Tiny details, big questions

Edinburgh. Freedom. Great!
Well, you'd have thought so. But it wasn't quite.

Yes, he loved the city, with the planned order of the new town and the higgledy-piggledy of the old town – 'Aud Reekie'.

He loved the country round about – Arthur's Rock, the castle, the Pentland Hills and the deep sea beyond.

25

He loved the people, always questioning, taking nothing for granted. And the plays and operas at the Theatre Royal.

And oh, he loved the food: herrings, fried oysters, cod's head with oatmeal...

But he HATED the medicine. When he watched in the operating theatres, he thought the sight of blood was a fearful thing. And when he had to dissect dead bodies – he threw up.

Before long, he was sure.

HE'D NEVER BE A DOCTOR!

Does that mean going to Edinburgh was a waste of time?
Oh, no. Far from it.

He walked along the coastline and collected cuttlefish and
sea slugs, sponges and polyps.

He met a traveller, Charles Waterton, who'd been all over
the world and told Charles what it was like in tropical
rainforests. He also told him what a terrible thing slavery was.
Waterton had brought a freed black slave back with him, John
Edmonstone. John was a wonderful taxidermist – he stuffed
animals – and taught the art to Darwin.

Charles listened to professors saying outrageous things
which went against everything he had been brought up to
believe. The minds of the lower creatures were really just the
same as humans', and so were most of their organs, so there
was nothing special about us. One of these professors Charles
got on very well with – Professor Grant.

"Study tiny detail but ask big questions," Grant told Charles.
And he never forgot it.

For the first time, Charles heard of an aged Frenchman, called
Lamarck. He said shocking things as well. He'd spent his life

looking at insects, worms, shellfish – and had decided that living creatures weren't fixed forever. One sort of creature could develop into another. The Church hated Lamarck. God had made every creature, they said. Nothing would ever change.

But Professor Grant told Darwin, "Don't listen to them. Lamarck is right."

And Charles began to listen.

Did Darwin not believe in God, then?
Of course he did. Big sister Caroline kept writing to him telling him to. Besides, he had to do something with his life.

He knew he wasn't going to be a doctor. But there was something he really could be.

A CLERGYMAN!

Yes, a lovely life as a vicar, with a nice vicar's wife and a nice vicar's house in an English village where he could wander round collecting insects to his heart's content – that would be *great*!

But how should he set about it?

Study somewhere else, I suppose.
Dead right. And if you wanted to be a clergyman there were only two places to choose from.

OXFORD OR CAMBRIDGE.

This was because in those days you could only go to either university if you were in the Church of England.

So he left Edinburgh and went to –

CAMBRIDGE.

A sleepy, windy little town on the edge of the wide, flat fens where rich young men went to have a smashing time and poor young men went to work their socks off.

Just like Oxford. Over the years, some things stay the same.

But in one way it was not like Oxford. Cambridge was a place of SCIENCE. It was then and it is now. As I said, some things stay the same.

In 1828, Charles Darwin went to Christ's College, Cambridge. But before that, something important happened.

CHAPTER FIVE

★   ★   ★   ★

A professor, a brown owl, a beetle and a girlfriend

Something important? What could that be?

It was all very well being a vicar in a nice house, but it wouldn't be much cop without a nice vicar's wife. And back at home, three months before he went to Cambridge, he met:

FANNY OWEN!

"Aha!" he said to himself.

She was small and slim, with dark eyes and raven-black hair. She was lively. She flirted a lot and rode horses superbly. Charles took one look and said – "This is the girl for me."

So he got married, then.

No. He had to persuade her father first. Squire Owen was not going to let any hopeless young man run off with his daughter. Fanny's suitor had to have PROSPECTS.

Was being a country parson good enough?

Well, Fanny seemed to think so.

In all the many letters she wrote to him, she called him her 'postillion' – a sort of coachman – while she called herself his 'housemaid'. Everything seemed great.

You are my.... tinker....tailor...Soldier.. GOT IT....POSTILLION!

No wonder Charles thought it was all sorted. But perhaps it wasn't yet.

Which was Darwin when he was at Cambridge – a rich boy having a terrific time or a poor boy working himself to death?
Neither. He didn't think much of the gambling, wine- and beer-swilling sons of dukes and lords. Also, to be a clergyman meant he didn't have to work very hard. He just had to get an ordinary Bachelor of Arts degree, the lowest Cambridge offered. A doddle.

So what did he do with his time?
He made good friends. Together, they had a great time. They formed a dining club called 'The Gluttons'. It had one aim – to eat food that nobody had eaten before.

Pictured here are some of the menus:

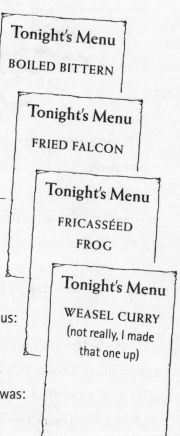

Tonight's Menu

BOILED BITTERN

Tonight's Menu

FRIED FALCON

Tonight's Menu

FRICASSÉED FROG

Tonight's Menu

WEASEL CURRY
(not really, I made that one up)

The Gluttons' Club was going well. Until, one evening , the main course was:

BROWN OWL.

They were so ill afterwards that the Gluttons' Club never met again.

But it didn't matter. A new interest was sweeping Cambridge:

ENTOMOLOGY!

Yes – butterflies, beetles, moths, more beetles – the Fens were full of them and Charles and his friends went chasing them. To good effect – they turned up several unknown species, killed them, brought them back to the college and set about identifying them.

Why?

Because science then was all about collecting and identifying species. The more people knew, the more they could wonder at God's wonderful creation. New species were identified all the time.

Nobody dared think they might have developed from old species. Oh no. Here, in solid Church of England Cambridge, the Bible meant exactly what it said and the world WAS created in seven days.

A great day came. Charles found a beetle people thought only lived in Germany. This was only the second time it had ever been found in Britain. Who could he tell?

There was only one person. Professor Henslow, professor of botany but known to be brilliant at *everything*, very young compared with the rest of the Cambridge dons, who thought for himself and let nobody tell him what to do – even though he was a clergyman himself.

And thus began a friendship which lasted all their lives and had tremendous consequences.

What were they?
Wait and see. Meanwhile the three years passed pleasantly, and Cambridge came and went. Soon he would be a vicar.

He didn't worry about the science, what Professor Grant once told him in Edinburgh or what Lamarck said. He'd just read William Paley, a clergyman and scientist who wrote a brilliant book showing just how superbly God had designed the world and everything in it. What a great man, Charles thought. He couldn't possibly doubt now that everything had been created by God as part of a huge and wonderful plan.

How happy he was. He'd find a village to be vicar of, carry on with his collecting and see about marrying Fanny. But meanwhile, before he did anything else, he went on a big walking tour of North Wales, collecting as he went, looking at strange rock formations and wondering why God had made them like that. He only had one regret. He'd wanted to organize a ship to take all his beetle-hunting friends to Tenerife, that untouched, unspoilt tropical island, to explore the wildlife there. It didn't come off and Wales had to do instead.

But when he came home, he found a letter from Professor Henslow that would change his life.

More than that. It would change the whole world.

CHAPTER SIX

★   ★   ★   ★

Sailing on the *Beagle*

Whatever could it be?

It was a invitation to go to sea.

So he'd get to Tenerife after all?

No. In fact he'd go almost everywhere *but* Tenerife. He was being asked to sail around the whole world.

Who by?

The Navy.

What had Charles Darwin got to do with the Navy?

Absolutely nothing.

I don't understand.

I'm not surprised. The captain's name was Fitzroy. The *Beagle* was a very tiny ship. Navy discipline then meant he couldn't be friendly with his juniors, so he had nobody to talk to. The last captain of the *Beagle* had killed himself through loneliness. Fitzroy didn't want to go the same way.

He asked his friend, Captain Beaufort at the Admiralty, to find someone he'd get on with to be his guest on the voyage. Beaufort asked Professor Henslow. Henslow thought of Darwin. Meanwhile, Captain Beaufort went on inventing the

Beaufort Scale, which is still used to measure the strength of gales.

The *Beagle* was a survey ship. Its job was to chart all harbours British ships were likely to go to and to find out as much as possible about far-off lands still unknown in Britain. Then we could trade with these countries, start church missions there – perhaps one day make them part of the British Empire. Fitzroy was a naturalist as well as captain. Darwin would be good company.

BUT – the voyage would last for years.

In the end, it took SIX.

What do you think Darwin said?

a) Did he say, "No way. I want to be a vicar. Besides, I've never been on a ship and I'd be seasick"?

b) Did he say, "No thanks. I want to marry Fanny and collect English beetles"?

c) Did he say, "Great. This is my big chance. I'll discover new species, make my name and be a great scientist"?

He's obviously going to say c), otherwise you wouldn't have started this chapter.

Dead right. But **a)** and **b)** went through his head and worried him a lot. Besides, he wasn't the ship's naturalist. The *Beagle* already had one, a man called McCormick, who was also the surgeon. When Charles set sail, officially he was nobody. Why give up everything just so he could spend six years cooped up on this tiny ship talking to a ship's captain he'd never heard of? They might *hate* each other.

But then he thought of exotic animals and birds never before heard of, teeming insects, great plains, huge mountains, steaming jungles, freezing wastes, vast continents and tiny islands and said to himself, "I've got to go".

On December 27th, 1831, *HMS Beagle* set sail from Plymouth, a little sailing ship on which there was hardly room to stand up.

So he didn't marry Fanny.

No. She'd been a bit distant lately. But when he left, he still had hopes.

And was he seasick?

Was he? He was terrible. He threw everything he'd ever eaten in his life back up over the ship's side. Perhaps the last bits of brown owl were among them.

Six years of this? Why did he start?

> I joined the Beagle
> To see the sea.
> And what did I see?
> I saw the sea.

Hold on, Charles. Things can only get better.

CHAPTER SEVEN

*   *   *   *

Right around the world – part 1

Which way first?

Fitzroy's orders were to make a survey of the coast of South America. So the *Beagle* headed west across the Atlantic.

SHIP'S LOG

300 miles west of Africa. Darwin has been seasick all the way.

Land sighted. Small island. St Jago. We will stop there.

Perhaps it will make him feel better.

Charles saw his first tropical plants on St Jago. He was amazed.

He saw something else too, which made him think. As he walked across the hot, dry plains, he saw a white band in the rock stretching for miles. It was made of corals and oyster shells, pressed hard together. But this was high above sea level. It must mean the sea had been there once. Why not now? Why had it gone? Had the Earth changed after all, or did God make it like that for some reason of his own?

St Jago was an old volcano. Did this mean that once upon a time this volcano had risen from the sea?

One man in the whole world thought so. He was back in London, his name was Lyell and he had written a book to say how the Earth's surface had gradually changed over millions of years. Not many believed him. They thought such ideas were shocking.

But Darwin looked at these shells high above the sea and said to himself, "*Lyell is right.*"

SHIP'S LOG

Atlantic crossed. Coast of Brazil in sight. Darwin has been seasick all the way. Still, he cheers up when he thinks about what he might find in South America.

Oh, the tropical forests and all the life in them fascinated Charles more than he could say. He started collecting specimens – plants, insects, animals. Especially insects. Weird creatures, like nothing ever even imagined before. They were preserved in alcohol, crated up and left in harbour for the next ship to take them back to England and Henslow. This was wonderful. But when they got to Rio, Charles had a *very nasty*

shock. Letters from home were waiting. Charles opened his, only to read that –

FANNY WAS MARRIED!

That was quick.

Well, there you go. A rich man hoping to go into Parliament had been hanging round a lot before Charles left. As soon as Charles was out of the way he had proposed, they were engaged in January and married in March.

What a thing to hear on the other side of the world! Charles was grief-stricken. It didn't cheer him up a bit when he found out she had a rotten time as a wife because her husband was a bullying rat.

Come on now, Charles. Forget Fanny and just concentrate on the voyage.

"Don't worry," said Charles bravely. "I will." And he did.

SHIP'S LOG

McCormick fed up. Wants to go home. Can't stand Darwin. So now we've got no naturalist and no surgeon either. Ah well, we'll just have to get on without him.

Is Darwin worth all this trouble? He is still seasick. Still, there is one thing. Now McCormick's gone, Darwin can be ship's naturalist.

The *Beagle* sailed on. And on. And on.

Where to?

South. Always south. Down the South American coast. The tropics were left behind.

> ## SHIP'S LOG
>
> Off coast of Patagonia. Getting colder.
> Skies grey. Darwin seasick again.
>   Tierra del Fuego — 'Land of Fire' —
> close to. We have work to do there and cargo
> to deliver. We must chart the coastline and
> set up a Mission Station.

Tierra del Fuego.

When they landed – no more forests. Bare, barren land. The very end of the world. This was where the *Beagle's* last captain killed himself.

What was the cargo Fitzroy had to deliver? Years before, three people were taken from their hard lives on Tierra del Fuego and brought to

England. They had been given English names – sort of. York Minster, Jemmy Button and Fuegia Basket. They had learned to speak English and act like English people. Surprise, surprise – they preferred this new comfortable life to their old one. When Darwin saw where they came from, he was shocked. He wrote: "How entire the difference between savage and civilized man is greater than between a wild and a domesticated animal."

Nowadays, an explorer would look a bit closer and see there was a culture as worthwhile as any others. But Darwin, like everyone else, thought that no being on Earth was higher than an English gentleman in the Church of England. That was why York, Jemmy and Fuegia were going back, with an English missionary. They would start a mission and turn the other Fuegians into Christian Englishmen, because they'd see at once it was the best way to be.

In this they were sadly mistaken. Why? Darwin found something to think about here which was very important.

What was it?
All in good time. Wait and see.

Now he wandered the Land of Fire. He looked at barren

shingly wastes and steep mountains, he found huge skulls and
bones of long-extinct animals – mastodons like huge
elephants, megatheriums like vast llamas, a gigantic armadillo
– and all the time he wondered – "How did they get here?"
He remembered the layer of shells all round St Jago. He'd just
read Lyell's latest book on geology. It said that landscapes
altered slowly, some parts rising out of the sea, others sinking
below them.

Perhaps, millions of years ago, everything here had been
very different.

When they got to Argentina, Charles spent months riding across the great plains – the Pampas – still finding fossils and specimens, seeing strange birds and animals not seen anywhere else in the world, fascinated by everything he came across.

Then back to Tierra del Fuego.

How were Jemmy, York and Fuegia getting on?
Terribly. Or so Darwin thought. They only found Jemmy. He was married. York and Fuegia had gone away. All were living as they had before – and were liking it. The missionary was fed up and wanted to come home.

"Why?" Darwin wondered. They'd lived a lovely life in

Britain, yet gone back to their old one. Why hadn't the Fuegians died out years ago in this cold, miserable land? Had they somehow adapted themselve to it over thousands and thousands of years? Perhaps they weren't so primitive after all.

Food for thought.

SHIP'S LOG

We have left Tierra del Fuego for ever. Round southern tip of South America, through Straits of Magellan and _NOT_ round Cape Horn. We're not stupid. Darwin more seasick than ever.

Turned north and sailed up coast of Chile. Days getting brighter and warmer. About time too. We'll dock first in Valparaiso. Plenty of British settlers there. Then we'll sail up the coast to Valdivia.

In Valdivia Darwin had three strange experiences. First – an orchard. Valdivia was surrounded by them. Trees grew very quickly here – all from little cuttings. Strange. Surely, he thought, if you cut a branch off a tree, it was part of that tree

and would die with it. But these cuttings didn't. They became new trees. Nobody had noticed that before. Perhaps all living things are like 'cuttings' from their parents.

Second – an earthquake. *The world, the very emblem of all that is solid, shuddered beneath our feet like a crust over fluid.* There was something to think about, because as a result – THE LAND HAD RISEN A FEW FEET. Lyell was right. Some land rose while other land sank – and not just because of earthquakes.

Third – one of the greatest things to happen to him on the whole voyage. He crossed the Andes and saw one of the great mountain ranges for the first time. How did it get there? What incredible forces had made it?

But now it was time to leave South America. Charles said goodbye to it forever – but what he had found there would never leave him.

★   ★   ★   ★

CHAPTER EIGHT

Right around the world – part 2

How long have they been away now?

It's 1835. They left Plymouth over three years before. Would
they ever get back? Yes. Before they left South America,
Fitzroy told them they'd be home in 18 months.

Now Darwin had to think about what he'd do when he came
back. But first –

SHIP'S LOG

Galapagos Islands sighted. What a dump.
Who'd want to live there?

Where?

A group of tiny islands in the Pacific, 600 miles off South
America. They were 'frying hot', black, dead volcanoes sticking
out of the sea. And on them – what strange wildlife! Turtles
swam in the bays, giant tortoises lumbered round the land,
'disgusting clumsy lizards' slept on the baking rocks. Strange
little birds like finches and bigger, uglier birds – sort of
mocking birds. No insects. Odd.

Stranger still – the four small islands were very close to each
other, but all the animals on them were different. Tortoises on

55

one island had different shells from those on the others. The birds were all different. So were the few trees – each tree unique to its own island.

In the end, what he saw on the Galapagos Islands was more important than anything else on the voyage. But he had no idea of that then. Why they were different would come much later. Meanwhile, the *Beagle* had loaded up with tortoises and Charles happily ate them all the way to Tahiti, while the cook threw the shells with their different markings overboard.

Charming. And pretty ignorant, really. Civilization was certainly spreading fast.

SHIP'S LOG

Near Tahiti. Darwin so excited that he forgot to be seasick. Wouldn't mind living here myself. Captain Cook even passed through here a few times on his travels, before he came to a sticky end in the Pacific islands...

Charles loved Tahiti and was most pleased to see the Tahitian people so Christian and civilized. Why couldn't Jemmy Basket and his friends have been the same?

DARWIN WAS SICK HERE.... AGAIN + AGAIN + AGAIN.

Where next?

New Zealand (he didn't like it) then Australia. He wasn't sure about Australia. It would be 'a great princess in the South' one day, he said, but it was 'too great and ambitious for affection yet not great enough for respect'.

He never went there again. Just as well really if that's what he thought.

But they were well on their way home now.

SHIP'S LOG

Approaching the Cocos Islands. Here our orders are to find out all we can about the coral reefs there. Will they be good harbours for British ships?
As well as that — WHAT ARE THEY?

Charles was very interested in the coral reefs. He saw the smooth waters of the lagoons, the thousands of tiny coloured fish, the intricate branchings of the coral – and asked himself why.

Here is the reason he came up with. Some land rises, other land falls. These were volcanoes which were slowly falling under the sea. But the coral, a living thing, had risen from the volcano's surface and formed a round wall in the sea inside which the water could be smooth and green.

When Darwin came home, he'd try to meet the great Lyell and ask him what he thought of his theory.

Next came Mauritius, then Capetown (where he met the great scientist and astronomer Sir John Herschel. He was in South Africa for two years to map the stars in clearer skies than he got at Greenwich), back into the Atlantic and St Helena, where Napoleon had been exiled.

Nearly home now, then.

Not yet. Disaster.

SHIP'S LOG

Left St Helena this morning. Compasses should be pointing north. Instead they point west-south-west. We shall have to sail back to Brazil to check the longitude. Crew not happy about this. Tough.
Darwin seasick again.

Charles was cheesed right off. "I loathe, I abhor the sea." he said.

However, the extra voyage didn't take long and now England neared. But Charles had so much to think about. What would he do when he came back?

What do you think Darwin would do? Would he:

a) Be a clergyman as he intended when he left?

b) Find a woman instead of Fanny to marry?

c) Try his luck at being a scientist?

What would stop him doing a)? He was all for being a clergyman when he left.

Ah, but he wasn't now. He'd seen a lot which made him think hard. Perhaps there wasn't a great plan behind nature. Perhaps the Earth hadn't been created in seven days. It was changing and developing all the time. Perhaps species of animals and plants weren't made and fixed forever by God. Perhaps they could change and develop as well. Perhaps it was their surroundings which made them what they were.

Oh, there was so much to think about. One thing was sure. William Paley's book must be wrong. And if that was so, he couldn't be a clergyman. Not then, in the 19th century.

Surely he couldn't do b) yet. Had he got over Fanny?

Perhaps he never really got over Fanny. But whether clergyman or scientist, he'd need a wife. Besides, his elder brother Erasmus hadn't married. If Charles didn't, who would pass on the Darwin name? He'd better find someone, quick.

He'd do c), wouldn't he?

Not easy. Nobody knew him after so long away. He'd had no proper scientific training. Before he left, he'd only been collecting things.

Besides, what if his crates of specimens hadn't got back? What if his ideas about corals, rocks, plant and animal species were laughed at? No, being a scientist was not going to be easy.

But he'd soon have to make up his mind.

SHIP'S LOG

October 2nd, 1836. This morning we docked in Falmouth.

The voyage of the Beagle is over. Said goodbye to Darwin. Not a bad sort of chap after all. And there's one good thing — DARWIN WILL NEVER BE SEASICK AGAIN.

★ ★ ★ ★ ★

CHAPTER NINE

The new life and marriage

What did his family think of him now?

They saw a different person – six years older, a lifetime wiser.

They could see he wasn't going into the church. His father gave him £400 a year to live on. Not much? In 1836, very comfortable indeed.

Besides, there was good news. All the specimens had got back, they were full of things nobody in Europe had ever seen before and:

DARWIN WAS A SENSATION!

So was he a famous scientist now?
Wait a minute. Where was he going to live? Not Shrewsbury, for sure. The back of beyond.

Cambridge? Henslow was there, but nobody else. Too church-dominated.

No, it had to be London. He'd stay with Erasmus – for now.

Meanwhile, he must meet people.

First, the great Lyell – who thought Charles was great as well and said he must be right about coral reefs.

Then Lyell introduced him to all the other scientists of London, at the British Museum, the Zoological Society. Charles met them, listened to them and realized –

He was making enemies as well as friends. There were some

who *hated* his theories. Especially when two fossils were found of monkeys millions of years old. "Aha," said Darwin. "Perhaps their tails dropped off in those millions of years and they developed into humans."

What a shocking thing to say. Being a scientist with new ideas was not going to be easy.

GOD DESIGNED EVERY LIVING THING
AND THERE WAS AN END OF IT.

That's what you would think if, let's say, you were very, very rich. You owned huge country estates and a big house in London. You were probably a Duke or an Earl – a Sir at the very least. That God had meant it this way was something you would take for granted.

Would you want someone coming along and saying, "The way you think the world was made may not be right after all?" No, you would not. NOTHING must ever change.

Ah, but what if you weren't rich or titled? Let's see.

The Evolution Quiz

Let's see where you stand in the argument.
Tick the box against the answer that best describes you.
*Score: 3 for **a**, 2 for **b**, 1 for **c**, 0 for **d**.*

1. You are:
   a. A duke. ☐
   b. A bishop, judge or some such. ☐
   c. A businessman on the make. ☐
   d. The poor twerp who does all the work. ☐

2. You live in:
   a. A castle. ☐
   b. A mansion, bishop's palace or an exclusive house in the best part of town. ☐
   c. A big house near your factory. ☐
   d. A tiny two up, two down same as all the rest in the street, one loo and pump for water between you all. ☐

3. You have as much money as:
   a. Your vast estates bring in without you doing a thing to earn any of it. Remember, you and your friends own most of Britain and Ireland. But you have no idea how much it is. ☐

b. However much you get as the huge salary you earn in your high profession.

c. You can, more and more each year you hope, from profits on your mill, factory, railway or whatever. ☐

c. Five shillings a week? You'll be lucky. ☐

4. When it comes to an election you vote for:

a. Whoever wants to keep things just as they are (e.g. The Duke of Wellington's Tories). ☐

b. Probably the same, though I'm open to argument. Or bribes. ☐

c. Anyone who'll let me get on and make whatever I want and do what I like without interfering (e.g. the Whigs). ☐

d. Vote? What's a vote? ☐

Well, how did you do?

If you scored 11–12, then it's long live the Church of England and may those scientists rot in hell. "God bless the squire and his relations and keep us in our proper stations," – that's the way to be.

9–10. If I thought that things might be a bit different, then perhaps I could get *right* to the top, along with those earls and such like.

8. Yes. The scientists are right. Just as things are not what we thought in nature all these years, they're not the same in Britain either. My father was nobody and I'm somebody, all by my own efforts. Nature's the same. If I can do better, so can animals. The game goes to the strong and the ruthless.

0. It doesn't matter what I think. Nobody hears.
(But they will, one day, they will).

Charles knew all this. The way his thoughts were beginning to take him made him VERY UNHAPPY INDEED.

So what did he do now?

For a start, he ought to get married. But who to?

Well, there were always his cousins, the Wedgwood girls. He really liked them. Especially the youngest, Emma. And lots of people married their cousins. What could be wrong with it? So, in November 1838 he plucked up courage and asked her.

MARRY ME... ..ER..... NO, THAT'S NOT THE RING!

He wasn't feeling well. He had a bad stomach which stayed with him for the rest of his life. But when Emma said "Yes," and seemed to wonder why he'd been so slow he felt much better. For a while.

BUT – Emma was very religious. Charles was wondering how he could ever believe in God again. Everything he saw took him away from what he was supposed to think. This kept him awake at night. How could he go on upsetting everyone he knew and loved? Was this what made his stomach so bad?

Anyway, on January 31st 1839, Charles married Emma and they settled in London, near the British Museum.

Was everything all right now?
Yes – but...

But what?
London seemed good for Charles. His work was there. All the scientific societies, museums and colleges were just down the road. How convenient.

Yet how awful. He never got a moment to himself. London was filthy. The streets were covered in horse dung. Emma didn't like it. Charles's stomach got worse. This was no place to have children.

What a year 1839 was. He got married, his book *The Voyage of the Beagle* came out, his first child was born. A son called William. In 1841, a daughter, Anne. Charles should be so happy.

But he was always ill, the arguments in science went on and he knew in his heart that EVOLUTION was right, whatever the bishops said, whatever other scientists thought, however much it upset Emma.

There were riots in the London streets. People with nothing were beginning to get very angry about being poor when others were so rich. Would there be a revolution?

The Darwins had to get away. In 1842, they managed it. They moved to the house they'd live in for the rest of their lives. The old parsonage in Down in Kent, very near to Bromley. Deep in the country. Perfect.

★　★　★　★

CHAPTER TEN

Life at Down House

Was everything all right now?
No. Emma was having her fourth baby – a girl called Mary
Eleanor. She only lived for a fortnight. Not a happy start.

Charles set up his study and worked hard. Books about rocks
and insects, plants and animals poured out. All of them had
the same idea behind them. Evolution.

But what made evolution work?

There was something more he had to find out. There were things he'd seen on the voyage of the *Beagle*, and especially in the Galapagos Islands that he couldn't quite get hold of. He wrote to his scientific friends, travelled to London for meetings, still couldn't quite understand. And he daren't write a book about all this. Not yet. The Church would hate it, nobody would speak to him, Emma would be very distressed.

Besides, someone had beaten him to it. In 1844, Robert Chambers from Edinburgh, not a scientist at all, wrote a book in which he outlined the whole evolution theory Darwin was working towards. He was horrified.

The book swept the country. Everyone was talking about it. Had he stolen all Darwin's glory?

No. Real scientists laughed at Chambers' book and Darwin knew why. It was only theory. Darwin knew his ideas were only theory as well. He had to prove them by long, hard experimentation. But on what?

Ah, he knew. Barnacles.

Do you mean those little shellfish which cling to the bottoms of boats?

Those are the ones. Down House was soon full of them, different varieties from all over the world. Darwin dissected them, peered at them through his microscope and wrote notes. All his time was spent locked up with barnacles. His children never thought this was strange. "Where does your father keep *his* barnacles?" they asked their friends in the village.

At last, Darwin had his answer. Some barnacles were equally male and female, some were more male, others more female, some were completely male, others were completely female. He was looking at evolution actually happening. First, both sexes were in the same creature, then they gradually developed so in the end each was of a different sex. Barnacles made him certain he was right. Evolution was true.

Now did he wrote a book about it?
No. He still didn't dare. His stomach got worse. He wrote out

his ideas and locked them away with a letter to Emma to publish them only after he was dead.

Why? Did he think he was going to die?
Yes, he did. And in 1850 came something much more terrible. Charles was so ill that he went to Malvern for a water cure. The whole family went as well. But his daughter Anne, his favourite child, took ill there. Nothing could save her. She died. She was nine years old.

Darwin was grief-stricken. "Is my illness passed on from generation to generation?" he wondered. And then, "Why have two of my children died so young when they want for nothing?"

A good question. He'd come back to it later, especially as Emma was now 43 and having her seventh child, a boy called Horace. Now perhaps the time had come. All his friends said so. He started his big book on the great idea –

NATURAL SELECTION.

What's that, then?
It means that, through the generations, species change by tiny little degrees that you don't notice. The ones which keep going are those which change so that they can survive in the

surroundings they live in. That's why wading birds have developed long legs, beaks and necks so they can stoop in the water, see fish, scoop them up and swallow them, while other birds have short, strong beaks to crack open shellfish or nuts. Creatures which adapt to where they live survive, those which can't, don't. Some animals thrive, others die out. Nature decides.

That was why tortoises and birds on one island in the Galapagos were different from those on others. They had stayed on their own island for millions of years, and adapted to those particular surroundings. Nothing ever came to upset them. Until man, that is.

Now Darwin wrote to farmers and animal breeders. They could make a new animal breed or a new strain of plant in a few generations with selective breeding. How did they do it? He started keeping pigeons and joined pigeon-fancying clubs, breeding pigeons with new combinations of colours and in different sizes. What he did in a few months, took nature millions of years. But nature did it in the end.

What about human beings?
Ah, yes. That was the big one. Had they developed from something else or were they really special and separate?

In 1857, an old enemy of Darwin's, Professor Owen, announced a discovery. He had studied the brains of apes and men. Human brains had an extra lobe in them, thus showing they were completely different from anything else.

Humans were different from any other creature. "I wonder," said Darwin, "what a chimpanzee would say to this?"

A WELL-KNOWN CHIMPANZEE REPLIES

Right. Listen up. You want to know what I think? Well. I'm disgusted with the lot of you. And I'm sad as well. I never thought I'd live to see such an ungrateful lot of grandchildren.
You think you're so great, don't you? Well, answer me this.

Wouldn't you be like to be able to climb trees and leap from branch to branch without a care in the world? Beats plodding round on the ground any day. You seem a right weak-kneed lot to me.

Wouldn't you like to be able to pick things up with your feet? Dead useful, that is, I'll tell you.

Wouldn't you like to be hairy ALL OVER, so you didn't have to waste time putting on those ridiculous clothes?

Wouldn't you like to be able to crack nuts with your bare hands?

And why isn't a nice pink bum good enough for you any more, answer me that?

Oh, it really grieves me to see you've thrown away nearly everything we tried to give you. I reckon it's been downhill all the way for you humans. I really worry about you sometimes. And let me give you a bit of advice. Don't let the gorillas hear what you think. They'd tear you limb from limb.

Yours more in sorrow than anger,

Charlie Chimp

"Well spoken, old friend," Darwin would have said if he'd read that. But he was too busy. All through the 1850s he experimented, observed and wrote. The GREAT BOOK was nearly finished. Then, in 1858, came –

THE GREAT BOMBSHELL.

CHAPTER ELEVEN

★　★　★　★

The Origin of Species

What was this bombshell?

A man called Alfred Russell Wallace. He was a poor man, but he'd read Chambers' book and Charles's story of the *Beagle's* voyage. He saved up enough money to sail first to the Amazon and later to Borneo, sending butterflies, beetles and birdskins back to collectors in London. He often wrote to Darwin and now he sent him a twenty-page letter in which he –

OUTLINED THE VERY SAME THEORY OF NATURAL SELECTION!

Poor Darwin. It looked as though someone was going to beat him to it. What could he do? Tear the letter up? Of course he couldn't.

Emma's eighth child, another Charles, was dying. Just as well, perhaps, they thought. This little Charles was very retarded. But Darwin was so full of grief that he couldn't think straight.

So he listened to his friends and did what they suggested. First, he outlined his own ideas and put them forward with Wallace's letter to a scientific meeting. So Wallace got some credit. But everybody now knew what Darwin really thought. He couldn't hide it any more.

He had to write a new book, shorter than the one he was doing, to put his ideas properly. He threw himself into work. He forgot his sadness over Anne and little Charles, he forgot the pain in his stomach and wrote and wrote and wrote. At last, in 1859, the great book was published:

ORIGIN of the SPECIES.

This is hard to swallow!

The Origin of Species.

And the world has never been the same since.

Why not?

If Wallace was a bombshell to Darwin, to the rest of the world Darwin was like a giant asteroid the size of the Moon crashing into the Atlantic.

Think of it. Here's someone saying: "I know what you've taken for granted for the last few thousands of years is WRONG. You'll all have to think again."

It seemed to mean the Church was wrong, all religion was finished, everything on which people based their lives was swept away by ONE LITTLE BOOK.

Oh, dear. What would poor Charles do now?

Everybody read *The Origin of Species*. Bishops were scandalized, and half the world with them. The other half rejoiced. Some said that from now on, Science ruled alone. Others said that Darwin had done the work of the devil.

"We'll sort him out," said the bishops.

"We'll sort *them* out," said the scientists.

As for Darwin, he kept quiet.

But the scene was set. The battle lines were drawn. And now even the battlefield was chosen. The 1860 Conference of the British Association for the Advancement of Science, to be held in Oxford.

THIS WOULD BE THE GREAT SHOWDOWN.

But who would win?

In the red corner, for the Church and everybody who thought Darwin was the voice of the devil –

SAM WILBERFORCE
Bishop of Oxford and great at maths.

In the blue corner, for Science and the new way of thinking –

THOMAS HUXLEY AND
JOSEPH HOOKER

Scientists and Darwin's friends,

who were sure he was right.

Just a minute. Where's Darwin?

At home nursing his stomach which was feeling *especially* bad just now – and scared stiff anyway. Anyway, here's what happened at the meeting.

THE DARWIN SUPPORTERS' CLUB FANZINE

Special Report

Great Struggle at the British Association
A SPECTATOR'S VIEW

I'll never forget the events of June 30th, 1860, at the New Museum in Oxford. Some have said it was the biggest victory since Waterloo, and if you are a Darwinian, you'll definitely agree.

The great day dawned. Long before the meeting, the lecture room was overflowing and still more were pushing in. We all had to move to a bigger hall. The battle started. Darwin's friend Professor Henslow was in the chair. Two more friends, Thomas Huxley and Joseph Hooker, were on the platform. First, were some minor speakers. But we hadn't come to hear them. They were so boring we booed them off the stage.

Then came the crunch. The audience round me was hushed as one man rose to speak. 'Soapy' Sam Wilberforce, The Bishop of Oxford, great scholar, great mathematician, would speak for the Church. His supporters stood up and waved their handkerchiefs. They thought Darwin and his dreadful book would be put where they belonged.

But Huxley and Hooker needn't have worried. Soapy Sam soon showed that *he didn't know what he was talking about*. He didn't even begin to understand the book. I mean, the things he said. Crazy. Listen to them:

Why were animals mummified by ancient Egyptians the same as ours? Why couldn't scientists turn one kind of animal into another? Then he had the cheek to ask Huxley whether he was descended from an ape on his mother's or his father's side. Well, I mean. Ignorant or what? Perhaps he'd never even read the book. I think Huxley knew the battle was won.

Soapy Sam finished. Huxley stood up. First, he answered Soapy's points one by one. Then he said, in words I won't forget:

"A man has no reason to be ashamed of having an ape as a grandfather. If there were an ancestor I should feel shame in recalling, it would be a man, endowed with great ability and splendid position, who should use these gifts to..."

HOLD THAT ONE, SOAPY!

Then Hooker really put the boot in... Game, set and match to the Darwinians. Yet guess what? Soapy Sam seemed to think he'd won! What a twerp. Some of his mates thought it was a draw. Not from where I was sitting it wasn't.

YOUR SPECIAL CORRESPONDENT

Sounds great. I bet Darwin wished he was there.

Well, he did and he didn't. Back at Down House, he read the letters that Huxley and Hooker sent him about the meeting. Yes, he was pleased. But he was also afraid. He knew the real battle hadn't even started.

He also felt guilty. Yes, he was too ill to stand up for himself, No, he didn't like to think that others had to do his fighting for him. But he still worried about what people would say about him 'doing the devil's work'. Besides, Emma didn't like it.

CHAPTER TWELVE

★　★　★　★

And afterwards?

Was there anything afterwards? What more was left for Darwin to say?

There was plenty. *The Origin of Species* made everyone latch on to the idea that humans were descended from monkeys. But shall I tell you something?

Go on.

Darwin never mentions that in *The Origin of Species*, even though people called it 'The Gorilla Book'. In fact, he never mentions man at all. The book is all about plants and animals.

Is that so?

Definitely. Still, don't worry. Darwin was thinking about it. And something else as well, which upset him very much.

What was that?

Marrying his cousin. No, he never regretted it. He loved Emma and she loved him. It was just that –

What?

All his experiments with pigeons and talks with breeders and all his observations showed him that the strongest stock came when the parents were widely separated by birth. Breeders did not like in-breeding among their animals. Cousins were very closely related in the same family. Could it be that he and Emma were transmitting all the weaknesses of their families into their children? Two had died, one was retarded, none had the restless mind that he had – or grandfather Erasmus had. Really, they were all a disappointment to him. Could it be his own fault? And if so, why?

It's in the genes, isn't it?

Dead right. The bigger the gene pool, the stronger the person – or animal, bird or whatever. We all know that and we don't have to be scientists. But Charles Darwin didn't.

That's a bit sad, isn't it? It means his theories don't matter anymore.

Dead wrong. The amazing thing is how modern genetic theory shows how accurate they were. Yet there was still a long way to go before they were accepted. The battle raged on, and on and on...

Meanwhile, back at Down House, Charles thought that, since everybody blamed him for something he hadn't really said, he'd better give a bit of thought to where humans came from.

So where did they come from?

They came from apes. They gradually learnt to stand upright, they gradually developed reason and insight, their brains gradually grew, tiny little advances until modern humans appeared. So there was no great 'divine spark'. Humans weren't fallen angels, they were incredibly modified monkeys.

From

THE CHARLES DARWIN SUPPORTERS' CLUB FANZINE

THE DESCENT OF MAN
by GuessWho?

Well, he's done it again, hasn't he? This'll shut those bishops up once and for all. All right, so what if we are descended from monkeys? I reckon we've done well to get where we have and it's *much* better than having been there to start with, as our religious friends seem to think. So come on, Soapy Sam and all your cronies. Put up or shut up and bow to the evidence. And let's hear no more from you.

From

THE JOURNAL OF THE SOAPY SAM APPRECIATION SOCIETY

THE DESCENT OF MAN
by an agent of the devil

Is there no end to this man's effrontery? Spitting in the face of God and denying the Bible is one thing, to say that humans are not unique and separate from the rest of the animal kingdom is something else and absolutely horrifying. Still, I suppose in these strange days we must put up with terrible things like this. Besides there are some in the Church today who are beginning to think he might be RIGHT. Including our own Sam Wilberforce himself.

So perhaps I'd better just shut up.

Meanwhile, a well-known chimpanzee writes:

Dear Humans,

Welcome aboard. I knew you'd see it my way.

Yours,

Charlie Chimp

Was there such a row this time over his new book?
No. It was all dying down. As more and more scientists came

to agree with him, so did the rest of the world. Just as well. Because Darwin was very ill. That awful stomach which had tortured him for most of his life was winning in the end. In 1882, worn out, he died at Down House, surrounded by his family.

He was 73 and now regarded as one of the most important people of the whole of the 19th century.

CHAPTER THIRTEEN

*　*　*　*

Where shall we bury Charles?

Why ask? Did it matter?

Yes, it did. Charles wanted to be buried at home in Down. So did Emma. His wishes should be obeyed, she said.

But others thought different. He was a great man now. He was Britain's foremost scientist, who had worked out a theory which the rest of the world had accepted.

There was only one place:

WESTMINSTER ABBEY.

Here all the great and the good of the land were finally deposited. Darwin, his friends said, should be among them.

And everyone agreed. Queen, Prime Minister, the archbishops. Yes, the rows with the Church of years before were quite forgotten.

So on 26th April, 1883, a solemn funeral procession took his body to the Abbey, and there you can still see his monument today.

A great man who changed the world. Pity he was so scared about doing it at all.

*　*　*　*

CHAPTER FOURTEEN

And now?

Does anybody now not believe him?

Quite a few. Some still believe it's all a load of lies. The Earth
really was made in seven days, about 6,000 years ago, and then
everything was washed away in a great flood, except Noah and
two of every kind of animal. They are called Creationists.

Do all religious people people believe that?

No. Remember how, right at the beginning we wondered
whether, in a sort of way, Darwin and the Bible could both be
right? Well, there are many who believe they are. They believe
that the story in the Book of Genesis, which is part of

Christianity, Judaism and Islam is a MYTH, which accounts for many things in a wonderful story. Other religions have their own creation myths. They remain wonderful stories and in them all is a nugget of truth.

But there's been so much new science since Darwin. Hasn't he been proved wrong by now?
A lot is clearer. Genetics has shown us how things work that Darwin couldn't understand at all.

But the basic idea, of natural selection, with nature modifying itself incredibly slowly as species adapt to new places and surroundings, remains the same.

And if nature develops, then society can develop as well. People needn't live in their 'proper stations' and women aren't inferior to men just because it's always been that way.

Change, change, change, always developing, always adapting. As with nature, so with the world we make for ourselves. Yes, Darwin didn't only change the way we see how nature works.

He changed the way we live as well.

★   ★   ★   ★